Stories of Sakka, Lord of Gods

Stories of

Sakka,
Lord
of Gods

From the Samyutta Nikaya

A translation into English from the Sinhala translation

by

Venerable Kiribathgoda Gnānānanda Thera

A Mahamegha Publication

Stories of Sakka, Lord of Gods,
from the Samyutta Nikāya.

A translation into English from the Sinhala translation by
Venerable Kiribathgoda Gnānānanda Thera

ISBN : 9789556870527

Computer Typesetting by

Mahamevnawa Buddhist Monastery, Toronto
Markham, Ontario, Canada L6C 1P2
Telephone: 905-927-7117
www.mahamevnawa.ca

Published by

Mahamegha Publishers
Waduwawa, Yatigaloluwa, Polgahawela, Sri Lanka.
Telephone: +94 37 2053300 | 77 3216685
www.mahameghapublishers.com
mahameghapublishers@gmail.com

Contents

The Suvīra Chapter

The Seven Noble Promises Chapter

The Sakka Chapter

Namo Tassa Bhagavato Arahato
Sammā Sambuddhassa!

Homage to the Blessed One, the Worthy One,
the Supremely Enlightened One!

The Suvīra Chapter

1. Suvīra Suttaṁ:
The Discourse about the Deity Suvīra

This is how I heard. One time the Blessed One was staying in the province of Sāvatthi in Jeta's park, Anāthapiṇḍika's Monastery. There the Blessed One addressed the monks saying, "Oh monks." "Bhante," those monks replied to the Blessed One. The Blessed One said this:

"Monks, once in the past the titans marched against the gods for battle. Then, monks, Sakka, lord of the gods, addressed Suvīra, a young god, thus: 'Dear son Suvīra, these titans are marching against the gods for battle. Go, dear son Suvīra, launch a counter-march against the titans.'

"The young god Suvīra replied to god Sakka saying 'Yes, I will gain you victory.' But he failed to follow god Sakka's order.

"Monks, for the second time, Sakka, lord of the gods, told Suvīra, the young god, thus: 'Dear son Suvīra, these titans are marching against the gods for battle. Go, dear son Suvīra, launch a counter-march against the titans.'

"The young god Suvīra replied to god Sakka saying 'Yes, I will gain you victory.' But he failed to follow God Sakka's order.

"Monks, for the third time, Sakka, lord of the gods, told Suvīra, the young god, thus: 'Dear son Suvīra, these titans are marching against the gods for battle. Go, dear son Suvīra, launch a counter-march against the titans.'

"The young god Suvīra replied to god Sakka saying, 'Yes, I will gain you victory.' But he failed to follow God Sakka's order.

"Then, monks, Sakka, lord of the gods, told Suvīra, the young god, a verse:

"'If you can achieve a happy goal without having any courage or making any effort, Suvīra, you do that and take me along with you.'

Suvīra:

"'If a lazy person who doesn't have any courage and does not do any work can achieve a prosperous goal, God Sakka, please tell me what that prosperous goal is.'

God Sakka:

"'If you can achieve a happy goal while being lazy or without making any effort, Suvīra, you do that and take me along with you.'

Suvīra:

"'God Sakka, if a person can reach a happy goal without doing any work, oh god Sakka, please tell

me about that happy goal which is sorrowless and
without despair.'

God Sakka:

"'If there exists a place anywhere where no work
is done, no one will live there. Suvīra, the way to
reach that place is to follow the path which leads
to Nibbāna. Suvīra, go there and take me along
with you.'

"So, monks, even Sakka, lord of the gods, experiencing the happy results of his own merit, exercising supreme
power and rulership over the Tāvatiṁsa gods praises courage and effort. Then monks, how much more would it be
fitting here for you, who have become monks in such a well
taught Dhamma and discipline, to arouse energy, struggle,
and strive for the attainment of unattained Arahantship, for
the realization of unrealized Dhamma, for the achievement
of unachieved Nibbāna."

2. Susīma Suttaṁ:
The Discourse about the Deity Susīma

This is how I heard. One time the Blessed One was staying in the province of Sāvatthi in Jeta's park, Anāthapiṇḍika's Monastery. There the Blessed One addressed the monks saying, "Oh monks." "Bhante," those monks replied to the Blessed One. The Blessed One said this:

"Monks, once in the past the titans marched against the gods for battle. Then, monks, Sakka, lord of the gods, addressed Susīma, a young god, thus: 'Dear son Susīma, these titans are marching against the gods for battle. Go, dear son Susīma, launch a counter-march against the titans.'

"The young god Susīma replied to god Sakka saying 'Yes, I will gain you victory.' But he failed to follow god Sakka's order.

"Monks, for the second time, Sakka, lord of the gods, told Susīma, the young god, thus: 'Dear son Susīma, these titans are marching against the gods for battle. Go, dear son Susīma, launch a counter-march against the titans.'

"The young god Susīma replied to god Sakka saying 'Yes, I will gain you victory.' But he failed to follow God Sakka's order.

"Monks, for the third time, Sakka, lord of the gods, told Susīma, the young god, thus: 'Dear son Susīma, these titans are marching against the gods for battle. Go, dear son Susīma, launch a counter-march against the titans.'

"The young god Susīma replied to god Sakka saying 'Yes, I will gain you victory.' But he failed to follow God Sakka's order.

"Then, monks, Sakka, lord of the gods, told Susīma, the young god, a verse:

"'If you can achieve a happy goal without having any courage or making any effort, Susīma, you do that and take me along with you.'

Susīma:

"'If a lazy person who doesn't have any courage and does not do any work can achieve a prosperous goal, God Sakka, please tell me what that prosperous goal is.'

God Sakka:

"'If you can achieve a happy goal while being lazy or without making any effort, Susīma, you do that and take me along with you.'

Susīma:

"'God Sakka, if a person can reach a happy goal without doing any work, oh god Sakka, please tell me about that happy goal which is sorrowless and without despair.'

God Sakka:

"'If there exists a place anywhere where no work is done, no one will live there. Susīma, the way to reach that place is to follow path which leads to Nibbāna. Susīma, go there and take me along with you.'

"So, monks, even Sakka, lord of the gods, experiencing happy results of his own merit, exercising supreme power and rulership over Tāvatimsa gods praises courage and effort. Then monks, how much more would it be fitting here for you, who have become monks in such a well taught Dhamma and discipline, to arouse energy, struggle, and strive for the attainment of unattained Arahantship, for the realization of unrealized Dhamma, for the achievement of unachieved Nibbāna.

3. Dhajagga Suttaṁ:
The Discourse about the Top of the Flag

One time the Blessed One was staying in the province of Sāvatthi, in Jeta's park, at Anāthapiṇḍika's Monastery. There the Blessed One addressed the monks saying, "Oh Monks." "Bhante," those monks replied to the Blessed One. The Blessed One said this:

"Monks, once in the past the gods and titans were preparing for battle. Then Sakka, lord of the gods, addressed the Tāvatiṁsa gods thus: 'Dear sirs, when the gods are in battle, if any fear, terror, or hair-standing-on-end arises, on that occasion you should look at the top of my flag. When you look up at the top of my flag, then any fear, terror, or hair-standing-on-end will pass away.

"'If you fail to look up at the top of my flag, then you should look up at the top of the flag of Pajāpati, king of gods. When you look up at the top of the flag of Pajāpati, king of gods, then any fear, terror, or hair-standing-on-end will pass away.

"'If you fail to look up at the top of the flag of Pajāpati, king of gods, then you should look up at the top of the flag of Varuṇa, king of gods. When you look up at the top of the flag of Varuṇa, king of gods, then any fear, terror, or hair-standing-on-end will pass away.

"'If you fail to look up at the top of the flag of Varuṇa, king of gods, then you should look up at the flag of Īsāna, king of gods. When you look up at the top of the flag of Īsāna, king of gods, any fear, terror, or hair-standing-on-end will pass away.'

"Monks, for those who look up at the top of the flag of Sakka, lord of the gods, or of Pajāpati, king of gods, or Varuṇa, king of gods, or Īsāna, king of gods, any fear, terror, or hair standing on end may pass away or may not pass away. What is the reason for this? Because Monks, Sakka, lord of the gods, is not free from lust, is not free from hatred, and is not free from delusion. He is subject to fear, terror, and fright, and is quick to flee.

"But, monks, I also say this to you: If you have gone to a forest, to the foot of a tree, or to an empty hut, if any fear, terror or hair-standing-on-end that should arise in you, on that occasion, you should recollect me thus: The Blessed One is an Arahant, supremely enlightened, accomplished in the true knowledge and conduct, well gone, knower of worlds, unsurpassed leader of persons to be tamed, teacher of gods and humans, the enlightened teacher, the Blessed One. Monks, when you recollect me, any fear, terror or hair-standing-on-end will pass away.

"If you fail to recollect me, then you should recollect the Dhamma thus: The Dhamma is well taught by the Blessed One, visible here and now, timeless, inviting one to come and see, applicable to oneself, understood by the wise each for himself. Monks, when you recollect the Dhamma, any fear, terror, or hair-standing-on-end will pass away.

"If you fail to recollect the Dhamma, then you should recollect the Saṅgha thus: Of pure conduct is the community of disciples of the Blessed One. Of upright conduct is the community of disciples of the Blessed One. Of wise conduct is the community of disciples of the Blessed One. Of generous conduct is the community of disciples of the Blessed One. Those four pairs of persons, the eight kinds of individuals—that is the community of disciples of the Blessed One. They are worthy of offerings, they are worthy of hospitality, they are worthy of gifts, they are worthy of reverential salutations, the unsurpassed field of merit for the world. Monks, when you recollect the Saṅgha, any fear, terror, or hair-standing-on-end will pass away.

"What is the reason for this? Because, monks, the Tathāgata, the Arahant, the Supremely Enlightened One is free from lust, is free from hatred and is free from delusion; he is not subject to fear, terror and fright. He will never flee."

This is what the Blessed One said. Having said this, the Well Gone One, the Great Teacher, further said this:

"Oh monks, in a forest or at the foot of a tree, or in an empty hut, you should recollect the Supreme Buddha. Then no fear will arise in you.

"But if you fail to recollect the Supreme Buddha, leader of the world, the best of humans, then you should recollect the Dhamma, which is well expounded and leads to Nibbāna.

"But if you fail to recollect the Dhamma, which is well expounded and leads to Nibbāna, then you should recollect the Saṅgha, the unsurpassed field of merit.

"Monks, for those who recollect the Buddha, the Dhamma, and the Saṅgha, any fear, terror or hair-standing-on-end that should arise in them will surely pass away."

4. Vepacitti:
The Discourse about Vepacitti

At Sāvatthi. The Blessed One said this:

"Monks, once in the past the gods and the titans were prepared for battle. Then Vepacitti, lord of the titans, addressed the titans thus: 'Dear sirs, now there will be a battle between the gods and titans. If the titans win and the gods are defeated, tie up Sakka, lord of the gods, by his hands, legs, and neck, and bring him to me in the city of titans.'

"Monks, Sakka, lord of the gods, also addressed the Tāvatiṁsa gods thus: 'Dear sirs, now there will be a battle between the gods and titans. If the gods win and the titans are defeated, tie up Vepacitti, lord of the titans, by his hands, legs, and neck, and bring him to me in the Sudhammā assembly hall.'

"Monks, in the battle that followed, the gods won and the titans were defeated. The Tāvatiṁsa gods bound Vepacitti by his hands, legs, and neck, and brought him to Sakka in the Sudhammā assembly hall. When Sakka was entering and leaving the assembly hall, Vepacitti, bound by his hands, legs, and neck, scolded and insulted Sakka with rude, harsh words.

"Then monks, God Mātali, Sakka's charioteer, asked Sakka, lord of the gods, a question in verse:

> "'God Sakka, listening to the harsh words of Vepacitti, why do you put up with him so patiently? Is it because you are scared or because you are weak?'

God Sakka:

> "'It is not because I am scared or weak that I am patient with Vepacitti. How can a wise person like me have combat with a fool?'

Mātali:

> "'Fools will be angrier and try to fight if no one will keep them in check. That is why, with severe punishment, the wise man restrains the fool.'

God Sakka:

> "'I think that when one knows others are angry, if one mindfully maintains one's peace, that is the best way to control the fool.'

Mātali:

> "'God Sakka, I see the fault of that patience. When one is patient, the fool thinks of that person thus, "He endures me out of fear."

"'The fool will cause more trouble to the patient one, as a herd of bulls charges towards one who flees.'

God Sakka:

"'It doesn't matter whether one thinks or not, "He endures me out of fear." There is great benefit in cultivating good qualities within oneself. There is nothing better than patience.

"'Even though the strength of a fool is called power, in reality there is no power there. No one can challenge the patience of the one who is guarded by Dhamma.

"'If one gets angry at another angry person, he makes things worse for himself. The one who doesn't repay an angry person with anger, he wins the hard battle.

"'Knowing that his foe is angry, when one mindfully maintains his peace, he practices for his own welfare and the other's.

"'When he acts for the welfare of himself and the other, the people who are unskilled in the Dhamma consider the patient person a fool.'

"So monks, even Sakka, lord of the gods, experiencing the happy results of his own merit, exercising supreme power and rulership over Tāvatiṁsa gods praises patience and gentleness. Then how much more would it be fitting here for you who have become monks in such a well taught Dhamma and discipline to be patient and gentle."

5. Subhāsita Jaya Suttaṁ: Victory by Well-Spoken Words

At Sāvatthi. "Monks, once in the past the gods and the titans were prepared for battle. Then Vepacitti, lord of the titans, said to Sakka, lord of the gods:

"'Lord of the gods, let there be victory by well-spoken words.'

"'Yes, Vepacitti, let there be victory by well-spoken words.'

"Then, monks, the gods and the titans appointed a panel of judges saying, 'They will decide what has been well spoken and badly spoken by us.'

"Then, monks, Vepacitti, lord of the titans, said to Sakka, lord of the gods: 'Speak a verse, lord of the gods.'

"Monks, when this was said, Sakka, lord of the gods, said to Vepacitti, lord of the titans: 'Vepacitti, since you came into this world before me, you Vepacitti, speak a verse.'

"When this was said, Vepacitti, lord of the titans, spoke this verse:

"'Fools will be angrier and try to fight if no one will keep them in check. That is why with severe punishment the wise man restrains the fool.'

"Monks, when Vepacitti, lord of the titans, spoke this verse, the titans applauded, but the gods were silent.

"Then, monks, Vepacitti, lord of the titans said to Sakka, lord of the gods: 'Speak a verse now, lord of the gods.'

"When this was said, Sakka, lord of the gods, spoke this verse:

> "'I think, when one knows others are angry, if one mindfully maintains one's peace, that is the best way to control the fool.'

"Monks, when Sakka, lord of the gods, spoke this verse, the gods applauded but the titans were silent.

"Then, monks, Sakka, lord of the gods, said to Vepacitti, lord of the titans: 'Speak a verse, Vepacitti.'

"When this was said, Vepacitti, lord of the titans, spoke this verse:

> "'God Sakka, I see the fault of that patience. When one is patient, the fool thinks of that person thus, "He puts up with me out of fear." The fool will cause more trouble to the patient one, as a herd of bulls charges towards one who flees.'

"Monks, when Vepacitti, lord of the titans, spoke this verse, the titans applauded but the gods were silent.

"Then, monks, Vepacitti, lord of the titans, said to Sakka, lord of the gods: 'Speak a verse, lord of the gods.'

"When this was said, Sakka, lord of the gods, spoke these verses:

"'It doesn't matter whether one thinks or not, "He puts up with me out of fear." There is great benefit in cultivating good qualities within oneself. There is nothing better than patience.

"'Even though the strength of a fool is called power, in reality there is no power there. No one can challenge the patience of the one who is guarded by Dhamma.

"'If one gets angry at another angry person he makes things worse for himself. The one who doesn't repay an angry person with anger, he wins the battle hard to win.

"'Knowing that his foe is angry, when one mindfully maintains his peace, he practices for his own welfare and the other's.

"'When he acts for the welfare of himself and the other, the people who are unskilled in the Dhamma consider the patient person a fool.'

"Monks, when these verses were spoken by Sakka, lord of the gods, the gods applauded but the titans were silent.

"Then, monks, the panel of judges appointed by the gods and the titans said this:

"'The verses spoken by Vepacitti, lord of the titans, are dealing with punishment and violence. Those verses talk about things such as, "This is how punishments should be given, conflicts arise and the battle begins."

"'But the verses spoken by Sakka, lord of the gods, are dealing with non-punishment and non-violence. Those verses talk about things such as, "This is how to stop punishments, living in harmony and ending the battle." In conclusion, Sakka, lord of the gods, has won the victory by well-spoken words!'

"In this way, monks, Sakka, lord of the gods, won the victory by well-spoken words."

6. Kulāvaka Suttaṁ: The Bird Nests

At Sāvatthi. "Monks, once in the past the gods and the titans were in battle. In that battle the titans won and the gods were defeated. Monks, in defeat, the gods fled towards the north while the titans chased after them. Then, monks, Sakka, lord of the gods, addressed his charioteer Mātali in verse:

"'Watch out, O Mātali, there may be bird nests in the silk-cotton woods. Avoid them and turn the chariot back. Let's surrender our lives to the titans rather than make these birds be without nests.'

"'Yes, as you wish lord,' Mātali the charioteer replied, and he turned back the chariot with its team of one thousand of the best horses.

"Then, monks, it occurred to the titans: 'Now that Sakka's chariot with its team of one thousand of the best horses has turned back, it seems that the gods will have a battle with the titans for a second time.' Struck by fear, they fled to the city of the titans. In this way, monks, Sakka, lord of the gods won a victory by righteousness itself."

7. Na Dubbhiya Suttaṁ: One Should Not Betray

At Sāvatthi. "Monks, once in the past when god Sakka, lord of the gods, was alone, the following thought arose in his mind: 'Though someone may be my sworn enemy, I should not do wrong even against him.'

"Then, monks, Vepacitti, lord of the titans, having known with his own mind the thought in god Sakka's mind, went to Sakka, lord of the gods. Sakka, lord of the gods, saw Vepacitti, lord of the titans, coming in the distance and said to Vepacitti, lord of the titans: 'Stop, Vepacitti, you've been caught!'

"'Dear Sir, don't you remember the idea that just occurred to you? Did you abandon that?'

"'Okay then Vepacitti, swear that you will not betray me.'

Vepacitti:

"'Whatever evil comes to a liar, whatever evil comes to an insulter of noble ones, whatever evil comes to a betrayer of friends, whatever evil comes to one without gratitude: that same evil touches the one who betrays you, Sakka, Sujā's husband.'"

8. Verocana Asurinda Suttaṁ: Verocana Lord of the Titans

At Sāvatthi, in Jeta's park. At that time, the Blessed was sitting in meditation where he would spend the day. Then Sakka, lord of the gods, and Verocana, lord of the titans, went to the Blessed One and stood at opposite door posts. Then Verocana, lord of the titans, recited this verse in the presence of the Blessed One:

> "A man should strive hard until his well-being has
> been achieved. One shines due to the achievement
> of his well-being: This is the word of Verocana."

God Sakka:

> "A man should strive hard until his well-being has
> been achieved. One shines due to the achievement
> of his well-being. There is nothing better than
> patience."

Verocana:

> "All beings achieve success here or there accord-
> ingly. All creatures live together considering that
> living together is supreme. One shines due to the
> achievement of his well-being: This is the word of
> Verocana."

God Sakka:

"All beings achieve success here or there accordingly. All creatures live together considering that living together is supreme. One shines due to the achievement of his well-being. There is nothing better than patience."

9. Araññāyatana Isi Suttaṁ: The Discourse about the Seers in the Forest

At Sāvatthi. "Monks, once in the past a number of good and virtuous seers had settled down in leaf huts in the forest. Then Sakka, lord of the gods, and Vepacitti, lord of the titans, approached those good and virtuous seers.

"Vepacitti, lord of the titans, put on his boots, bound his sword on tightly, and with an umbrella over his head, entered the monastery through the main gate. Then having disrespected those good and virtuous seers, left.

"But Sakka, lord of the gods, took off his boots, handed over his sword to others, lowered his umbrella, and entered the monastery through the back gate. He stood in the direction where the wind blew passing over those seers' bodies, raised his joined hands in reverential salutation, and paid homage to those good and virtuous seers.

"Then monks, those good and virtuous seers addressed Sakka in verse:

"'The odour of the seers long bound by their promises, spreading from their bodies, goes with the wind. Turn away from here, oh thousand-eyed god. For seers' odour is foul, oh god-king.'

Sakka:

"'Let the odour of the seers long bound by their promises, spreading from their bodies, go with the wind. We desire this odour, oh venerable sirs, as we do a garland of flowers on the head. The gods do not perceive it as repulsive.'"

10. Isayosamuddaka Suttaṁ: The Discourse about the Seers along the Shore of the Ocean

At Sāvatthi. "Monks, once in the past, a number of good and virtuous seers had settled down in leaf huts along the shore of the ocean. At that time the gods and the titans were prepared for battle. Monks, then it occurred to those good and virtuous seers, 'The gods are righteous, the titans unrighteous. Fear might come to us from the titans. Let us go to Sambara, lord of the titans, and ask him for a guarantee of safety.'

"Then, monks, just as quickly as a strong man extends his drawn-in arm or draws in his extended arm, those good and virtuous seers disappeared from their leaf huts along the shore of the ocean. Then they reappeared in the presence of Sambara, lord of the titans. Those good and virtuous seers addressed Sambara, lord of the titans, in verse:

"'We, the seers, have come to Sambara to ask him for a guarantee of safety. You can give us fear or safety. Do what you wish.'

Sambara:

> "'You are friends with our enemy, god Sakka, I will not guarantee your safety. Though you ask me for safety, I will give you only fear.'

The Seers:

> "'When we have asked for safety, you only give us fear. We accept your words. May you not be separated from fear!

> "'Whatever type of seed you sow, that is the type of fruit you gain. The doer of good gains good, the doer of evil gains evil. Son, you have sown a seed, therefore you will receive the fruit of that.'

"Monks, those good and virtuous seers put a curse on Sambara, lord of the titans. Then monks, just as quickly as a strong man extends his drawn-in arm or draws in his extended arm, those seers disappeared from the presence of Sambara and reappeared in their leaf huts.

"But, monks, after being cursed by those good and virtuous seers, Sambara, lord of titans, always wakes up horrified three times in the night."

The Seven Noble Promises Chapter

11. Deva Sattavatapada Suttaṁ: The Discourse about the Noble Promises of God Sakka

This is how I heard. One time the Blessed One was staying in the province of Sāvatthi, in Jeta's park, at Anāthapiṇḍika's Monastery.

There, the Blessed One taught this:

"Monks, in the past, when Sakka, lord of the gods, was a human, he practised the seven noble promises. Since he did that, he achieved the position of Sakka, lord of the gods. What were those seven noble promises?

1. As long as I live may I help my parents.
2. As long as I live may I respect the family elders.
3. As long as I live may I speak gently.
4. As long as I live may I not speak divisively.
5. As long as I live may I live at home without greediness, removing the stain of stinginess, open-handed, always ready to give, always free to help others, delighting in giving and sharing, and well organized in giving charity.
6. As long as I live may I speak the truth.
7. As long as I live may I be free from anger, and if anger should arise in me, may I remove it quickly.

"Monks, in the past, when Sakka, lord of the gods, was a human, he practised these noble seven promises. Since he did that, he achieved the position of Sakka, lord of the gods."

(A verse)

When a person supports his parents, respects the family elders, speaks gentle and pleasing words, does not speak divisive words, removes greediness, speaks truthfully, and controls their anger, the Tāvatiṁsa gods call him a truly superior person.

12. Dutiya Deva Sattavatapada Suttaṁ: The Second Discourse about the Noble Promises of God Sakka

One time the Blessed One was staying in the province of Sāvatthi, in Jetta's park, at Anāthapiṇḍika's monastery. There the Blessed One said to the monks:

"Monks, in the past when Sakka, lord of the gods, was a human being, he was a youth named Magha; therefore he is called Maghavā.

"Monks, in the past, when Sakka, lord of the gods, was a human being, he gave gifts before others gave theirs on every occasion; therefore he is called Purindada.

"Monks, in the past, when Sakka, lord of the gods, was a human being, he gave gifts in a well organized manner; therefore he was called Sakka.

"Monks, in the past, when Sakka, lord of the gods, was a human being, he gave houses; therefore he is called Vāsava.

"Monks, Sakka, lord of the gods, thinks a thousand matters in a moment; therefore he is called Sahassa-netta, Thousand-eyed.

"Monks, Sakka's wife is the titan-maiden named Sujā; therefore he is called Sujampati, Sujā's husband.

"Monks, Sakka, lord of the gods, lives in great luxury, practices supreme power and rules over the Tāvatimsa gods; therefore he is called lord of the gods.

"Monks, in the past, when Sakka, lord of the gods, was a human being, he practiced seven noble promises. Since he did that, he became god Sakka."

(A verse)

When a person supports his parents, respects the family elders, speaks gentle and pleasing words, doesn't speak divisive words, removes greediness, speaks truthfully, and controls anger, the Tāvatimsa gods call him a truly superior person.

13. Mahāli Sattavatapada Suttaṁ: The Discourse about the Noble Promises Given to Mahāli the Licchavi

This is how I heard. One time the Blessed one was staying in the Hall with Peaked Roofs, in the great woods, in the province of Vesāli. Then Mahāli the Licchavi went to the Blessed One, paid homage to the Buddha, sat down to one side and said to the Blessed One:

"Bhante, have you ever seen Sakka, lord of the gods?"

"Yes Mahāli, I have seen Sakka, lord of the gods."

"Surely Bhante, the one that Bhante has seen must have been one who looked like Sakka. Bhante, Sakka, lord of the gods, is difficult to see."

"Mahāli, I know god Sakka, and I know qualities that make someone the god Sakka, and I also know by practicing which noble promises one achieves the status of god Sakka.

"Mahāli, in the past, when Sakka, lord of the gods, was a human being, he was a youth named Magha; therefore he is called Maghavā.

"Mahāli, in the past, when Sakka, lord of the gods, was a human being, he gave gifts before others gave theirs on every occasion; therefore he is called Purindada.

"Mahāli, in the past, when Sakka, lord of the gods, was a human being, he gave gifts in a well organized manner; therefore he is called Sakka.

"Mahāli, in the past, when Sakka, lord of the gods, was a human being, he gave houses; therefore he is called Vāsava.

"Mahāli, Sakka, lord of the gods, thinks a thousand matters in a moment; therefore he is called Sahassa-netta, Thousand-eyed.

"Mahāli, Sakka's wife is the titan-maiden named Sujā; therefore he is called Sujampati, Sujā's husband.

"Mahāli, Sakka, lord of the gods, lives in great luxury, practices supreme power and rules over the Tāvatiṁsa gods; therefore he is called lord of the gods.

"Mahāli, in the past, when Sakka, lord of the gods, was a human being, he practiced seven noble promises. Since he did that, he achieved the position of lord of the gods, Sakka."

(A verse)

When a person supports his parents, respects the family elders, speaks gentle and pleasing words, doesn't speak divisive words, removes greediness, speaks truthfully, and controls anger, the Tāvatiṁsa gods call him a truly superior person.

14. Dallidda Suttaṁ: The Discourse about a Poor Man

This is how I heard. At one time, the Blessed One was stay-ing in the province of Rājagaha in the Bamboo Garden, the Squirrels' Reserve. There the Blessed One addressed the monks saying, " Oh monks." "Bhante," those monks replied to the Blessed One.

"Monks, a long time ago, in this same province, there was a very poor and helpless beggar. He practiced faith, vir-tue, Dhamma learning, generosity, and wisdom in the path proclaimed by the Buddha. Having practiced faith, virtue, Dhamma learning, generosity, and wisdom in the path pro-claimed by the Buddha, after death, at the breakup of the body, he was reborn among the Tāvatiṁsa gods. He out-shone the other gods in regards to beauty and glory.

"Then monks, the Tāvatiṁsa gods became annoyed with him, criticized and insulted him saying, 'It is wonderful indeed sirs! It is amazing indeed sirs! For before he became a god, he was a poor helpless beggar. After death, at the breakup of the body, he was reborn among the Tāvatiṁsa gods, and now he outshines the other gods in regards to beauty and glory.'

"Then, monks, Sakka, lord of the gods, told the Tāvatiṁsa gods: 'Dear sirs, don't insult this god. In the past, this young god was a human being. He practiced faith, virtue, Dhamma learning, generosity, and wisdom in the path proclaimed by the Buddha. Having developed faith, virtue, Dhamma learning, generosity, and wisdom in the path proclaimed by the Buddha, after death he was reborn among the Tāvatiṁsa gods. He now outshines the other gods in regard to beauty and glory.'

"Then, monks, Sakka, lord of the gods, recited these verses, making the Tāvatiṁsa gods happy:

"'When one has unshakable, well established faith in the Supreme Buddha and good virtue, praised by the noble ones;

"'When one has confidence in the community of monks and one understands the Dhamma, they say that one isn't poor; his life is not meaningless.

"'Therefore the wise person, remembering the Buddha's teachings, should be devoted to faith, virtue, confidence and realization of the Dhamma.'"

15. Rāmaneyyaka Suttaṁ: A Delightful Place

At Sāvatthi, in Jeta's Garden, Sakka, lord of the gods, went to the Blessed One, paid homage to the Buddha and stood to one side. Standing to one side, he asked the Blessed One a question, "Bhante, what is really called the delightful place?"

The Blessed One:

"There are well constructed shrines, woodland shrines, parks, and lotus ponds. These are not worth one sixteenth of a delightful human being.

"Whether in a village or forest, in a valley or on the plain, wherever the liberated ones live is truly a delightful place."

16. Yajamāna Suttaṁ:
The Discourse about Sacrifices

At one time, the Blessed One was staying at the province of Rājagaha, on Mount Vulture Peak. Then Sakka, lord of the gods, went to the Blessed One, paid homage to the Buddha and stood to one side. Standing to one side Sakka, lord of the gods, asked the Blessed One a question in verse:

"For those people who make sacrificial offerings, searching for merit, to whom should they give to gain great results?"

The Blessed One:

"The community of monks consists of four types of disciples practising the path and four others who attained the fruit. These wise and virtuous disciples follow the straightway.

"For those people who make sacrificial offerings, searching for merit, the gift given to the community of monks generates great results."

17. Vandanā Suttaṁ:
The Discourse about Veneration

At Sāvatthi. Now at that time the Blessed One was sitting in meditation during the day. Then Sakka, lord of the gods, and Brahma Sahampati went to the Supreme Buddha and stood at opposite doorposts. Then Sakka, lord of the gods, recited this verse in the presence of the Blessed One:

"Rise up, O hero, victor in battle with Māra. The great being who released the burden of the aggregates! Oh the debt-free teacher! Wander in the world! Your well liberated mind is like the shining full moon in the night."

Brahma Sahampati: "It is not in such a way that the Tathāgatas are to be venerated, lord of the gods. The Tathāgatas are to be venerated, lord of the gods, thus:

"Rise up, O victor in Battle with Mara! O caravan leader who makes the beings cross over Saṁsāra! O debt-free teacher! Wander in the world! Teach the Dhamma, O Blessed One: there will surely be those who will understand."

18. Sakka Namassana Suttaṁ: The Discourse about the Worship of Sakka

At Sāvatthi. There, the Blessed One said this: "Monks, once in the past Sakka, lord of the gods, addressed his charioteer, Mātali, thus: 'Mātali, prepare the chariot with its team of a thousand of the best horses. Let us go to see the beautiful park.' Then, monks, the charioteer Mātali replied to Sakka, lord of the gods, saying, 'Yes sire, as you wish.' Then he prepared the chariot with its team of a thousand of the best horses and told Sakka, lord of the gods, 'The chariot has been prepared, my lord. You may come at your own convenience.' Then, monks, Sakka, lord of the gods, while coming down from Vejayanta Palace, put his hands together and worshipped all directions. Then, monks, Mātali the charioteer asked Sakka, lord of the gods, in verse:

"'They all humbly worship you—those well learnt in the Triple Veda, all the kings ruling on earth, the Four Great Kings, and the glorious Tāvatiṁsa gods—so who, O Sakka, is that god you worship?'

Sakka:

> "'These beings all humbly worship me—those
> well learnt in the Triple Veda, all the kings ruling
> on earth, the Four Great Kings, and the glorious
> Tāvatimsa gods—but I worship monks who are
> virtuous, long trained in the stillness of mind, and
> who live with the celibate life as their intention.

> "'There are householders who went for refuge to
> the triple gem, and have become lay followers of
> the Supreme Buddha. They are virtuous, make
> merit and righteously take care of their families. I
> worship them as well, Oh Mātali.'

Mātali:

> "'Those you worship, my lord Sakka, are indeed
> the best in the world. I too will worship them—
> those you worship, lord Sakka.'"

(The verse recited by the liberated ones in the first council:)

> "Having answered the question, having worshiped
> all directions, the king of gods—Magha, Sujā's hus-
> band, God Sakka—climbed into his chariot."

19. Dutiya Sakka Namassana Suttaṁ: The Second Discourse about the Worship of Sakka

At Sāvatthi. There, the Blessed One said this: "Monks, once in the past Sakka, lord of the gods, addressed his charioteer, Mātali, thus: 'Mātali, prepare the chariot with its team of a thousand of the best horses. Let us go to see the beautiful park.' Then, monks, the charioteer Mātali replied to Sakka, lord of the gods, saying, 'Yes sire, as you wish.' Then he prepared the chariot with its team of a thousand of the best horses and told Sakka, lord of the gods, 'The chariot has been prepared, my lord. You may come at your own convenience.' Then, monks, Sakka, lord of the gods, while coming down from Vejayanta Palace, put his hands together and worshipped all directions. Then monks, Mātali the charioteer asked Sakka, lord of the gods, in verse:

"'Both devas and human beings humbly worship you, Vāsava. So who, Oh Sakka, is that god you worship?'

Sakka:

> "'Oh Mātali, the perfectly enlightened Buddha lives in this world with its gods, the Great Teacher of perfect name: he is the one I worship.

> "'Oh Mātali, there are enlightened ones, free from taints, who have eradicated lust, hatred, and ignorance. These are the ones I worship.

> "'Oh Mātali, there are noble disciples doing proper duties who have gone beyond lust, hatred and ignorance. They live practicing the Dhamma, giving it top priority. These are the ones I worship.'

Mātali:

> "'Those you worship, my Lord Sakka, are indeed the best in the world. I too will worship them—those you worship, Lord Sakka.'"

(The verse recited by the liberated ones in the first council:)

> "Having answered the question, having worshiped the Blessed One, the king of gods—Magha, Sujā's husband, God Sakka—climbed into his chariot."

20. Tatiya Sakka Namassana Suttaṁ: The Third Discourse about the Worship of Sakka

At Sāvatthi. There, the Blessed One said this: "Monks, once in the past Sakka, lord of the gods, addressed his charioteer, Mātali thus: 'Mātali, prepare the chariot with its team of a thousand of the best horses. Let us go to see the beautiful park.' Then, monks, the charioteer Mātali replied, 'Yes sire, as you wish,' to the god Sakka. Then he prepared the chariot with its team of a thousand of the best horses and told Sakka, lord of the gods, 'The chariot has been prepared, dear sir. You may come at your own convenience.' Then, monks, God Sakka while coming down from Vejayanta Palace, put his hands together and worshipped the community of monks. Then monks, Mātali the charioteer asked Sakka, lord of the gods, in verse:

"'These people with dirty bodies worship you, they are stuck in these very same dirty bodies. They are badly affected with hunger and thirst.

"'God Sakka, they do not have homes and they are ascetics. Which conduct of those seers do you favour? We wish to hear what you have to say.'

Sakka:

"'Mātali, those seers who do not have homes, when they depart from a village, leave without any attachments. That is why I favour them.

"'They do not store things in a storage place, neither in a pot nor in a box; they survive by what is given to them by others. They are virtuous, wise and quiet. They only speak good words. They live peacefully.

"'While gods fight with titans, and people fight with one another, among those who fight, these seers do not fight. Among the violent, they are quenched. Among those who are attached to the world, they are not attached. Mātali, these are the ones I worship.'

Mātali:

"'Those you worshiped, my Lord Sakka, are indeed the best in the world. I too will worship them—those you worship, Lord Sakka.'"

(The verse recited by the liberated ones in the first council:)

"Having answered the question, having worshiped the community of monks, the king of gods—Magha, Sujā's husband, god Sakka—climbed into his chariot."

The Sakka Chapter

21. Jhatva Suttaṁ: The Discourse about Burning

This is how I heard. At one time, the Blessed One was staying in Anāthapiṇḍika's monastery at Jeta's garden in the province of Sāvatthi. Then Sakka, lord of the gods, went to the Blessed One, paid homage to the Blessed one and stood to one side. Then Sakka, lord of the gods, asked the Blessed One a question in verse:

"Oh venerable Gotama, what does one need to burn to sleep peacefully? What does one need to burn to not sorrow? What is the one thing whose killing you would approve?"

The Blessed One:

"Oh God Sakka, having burned anger one sleeps peacefully. Having burned anger one does not sorrow. The killing of anger with its poisoned root and honeyed tip (taking revenge) is the killing that the noble ones praise. Having burned anger indeed one does not sorrow."

22. Dubbanniya Suttaṁ:
The Discourse about Being Ugly

At Sāvatthi. There, the Blessed One said this: "Monks, once in the past a certain ugly and deformed demon sat down on the seat of Sakka, lord of the gods. At that time monks, the Tāvatiṁsa gods found fault with this, grumbled, and complained about it, saying, 'It is wonderful indeed sir! It is amazing indeed, sir! This ugly, deformed demon has sat down on the seat of Sakka, lord of the gods!'

"But to whatever extent the Tāvatiṁsa gods found fault with this, grumbled, and complained about it, to that extent the demon became more and more handsome, more and more attractive, more and more bright.

"Then monks, the Tāvatiṁsa gods went to Sakka, lord of the gods and said to him: 'Here, dear sir, an ugly, deformed demon has sat down on your seat. Then lord, the Tāvatiṁsa gods found fault with this and complained about it, saying: "It is wonderful indeed sir! It is amazing indeed, sir! This ugly, deformed demon has sat down on the seat of Sakka, Lord of the gods!" But lord, to whatever extent the Tāvatiṁsa gods found fault with this, grumbled, and complained about it, to that extent that demon became more and more handsome, more and more attractive, more and more bright.'

"'Oh sirs, that must be the anger-eating demon,' said Sakka. Then monks, Sakka, Lord of the gods, went to the anger-eating demon. Having gone, he put his upper cloth over one shoulder, knelt down with his right knee on the ground, and, putting his hands together worshiping respectfully the anger-eating demon, he said his own name three times: 'I, dear sir, am Sakka, lord of the gods! I, dear sir, am Sakka, lord of the gods!'

"To whatever extent Sakka, lord of the gods, said his name, to the same extent that demon became uglier and uglier and more and more deformed until he disappeared right there.

"Then, monks, having sat down on his own seat, instructing the Tāvatimsa gods, Sakka, lord of the gods, on that occasion recited these verses:

"'I am not one who hurts his own mind, nor is easily taken by anger. I have not gotten angry for a long time. Therefore anger does not stay in me.

"'When I'm angry I do not speak harshly, I only speak beneficial words. Seeing the benefit that comes to me from that patience, I always focus on my own faults.'"

23. Māyā Suttaṁ:
The Discourse about Magic

At Sāvatthi. There, the Blessed One said this: "Monks, once in the past Vepacitti, lord of the titans, was sick, afflicted, and seriously ill. Then Sakka, lord of the gods, went to Vepacitti to inquire about his illness. Vepacitti saw Sakka, lord of the gods, coming in the distance and said to Sakka, lord of the gods: 'Cure me, lord of the gods.'

"'If so, dear Vepacitti, teach me the Sambari magic.'

"'Dear sir, I won't teach it until I have asked the titans for permission.'

"Then, monks, Vepacitti, lord of the titans, asked the other titans: 'Sirs, may I teach the Sambari magic to Sakka, lord of the gods?'

"'No, lord, do not teach Sakka, lord of the gods, the Sambari magic.'

"Then, monks, Vepacitti, lord of the titans, told Sakka, lord of the gods, in verse:

"'O Sakka, king of gods, called Maghavā, Sujā's husband, people who do this magic will be reborn in the terrible hell and suffer there for a hundred years like it happened to the titan Sambara.'"

24. Accaya Suttaṁ: The Discourse about Offence

At Sāvatthi. At one time, two monks quarrelled, and one monk scolded the other monk loudly. Then the first monk confessed his offence to the other monk, but the second monk would not give him forgiveness.

Then a number of monks went to the Blessed One, paid homage to the Buddha, sat down to one side, and reported to the Blessed One: "Bhante, here, two monks quarreled, and one monk scolded the other monk loudly. Then the first monk confessed his offence to the other monk, but the second monk would not give him forgiveness."

"Monks, there are two kinds of fools: one who does not see an offence as an offence; and one who, when another is confessing an offence, does not give him forgiveness according to the Dhamma. Monks, these are the two kinds of fools.

"Monks, there are two kinds of wise people: one who sees an offence as an offence; and one who, when another is confessing an offence, gives him forgiveness according to the Dhamma. Monks, these are the two kinds of wise people.

"Monks, once in the past, Sakka, Lord of the gods, gladdening the Tāvatiṁsa gods in the Sudhammā assembly hall, on that occasion recited this verse:

"'Bring anger under your control! Do not let your friendship break! Do not blame those who are not worthy of blame! Don't speak divisive words! Anger crushes evil people, just like a mountain crushes beings.'"

25. Akkodha Suttaṁ:
The Discourse about Non-anger

At Sāvatthi. At one time, two monks quarrelled, and one monk scolded the other monk loudly. Then the first monk confessed his offence to the other monk, but the second monk would not give him forgiveness.

Then a number of monks went to the Blessed One, paid homage to the Buddha, sat down to one side, and reported to the Blessed One: "Bhante, here, two monks quarreled, and one monk scolded the other monk loudly. Then the first monk confessed his offence to the other monk, but the second monk would not give him forgiveness."

"Monks, there are two kinds of fools: one who does not see an offence as an offence; and one who, when another is confessing an offence, does not give him forgiveness according to the Dhamma. Monks, these are the two kinds of fools.

"Monks, there are two kinds of wise people: one who sees an offence as an offence; and one who, when another is confessing an offence, gives him forgiveness according to the Dhamma. Monks, these are the two kinds of wise people.

"Monks, once in the past, Sakka, Lord of the gods, gladdening the Tāvatiṁsa gods in the Sudhammā assembly hall, on that occasion recited this verse:

"'Do not let anger overpower you! Do not become angry at one who is angry! In noble ones' hearts there is always non-anger and harmlessness. But anger crushes evil people, just like a mountain crushes beings.'"

Mahamegha English Publications

Sutta Translations
Stories of Sakka, Lord of Gods
Stories of Heavenly Mansions
Stories of Ghosts

Dhamma Books
The Wise Shall Realize
The Life of the Buddha for Children

Childrens Picture Books
Chaththa Manawaka
Sumina the Novice Monk
Stingy Kosiya of Town Sakkara
Kisagothami
Kali the She-Devil
Ayuwaddana Kumaraya
Sumana the Florist

To order, go to www.mahamevnawa.lk